D1610971

The Rolling Stones

The Rolling Stones

DAVID CARTER

J G
PRESS

Published in the USA 1994
by JG Press
Distributed by World Publication, Inc.

The JG Press imprint is a trademark
of JG Press, Inc.
455 Somerset Avenue
North Dighton, MA 02764

Produced by
Brompton Books Corporation
15 Sherwood Place
Greenwich, Connecticut 06830

ISBN 1-57215-034-3

Printed in Slovenia

Page 2: **The youthful Rolling Stones.**

Above: **Early days, and hard to believe
such innocent looking lads would soon
be labeled the bad boys of
'rock 'n' roll'.**

CONTENTS

CHAPTER ONE

6. **Please allow me to
introduce myself**

CHAPTER TWO

10. **You can't always get
what you want**

CHAPTER THREE

20. **Satisfaction**

CHAPTER FOUR
28. **Get off of my cloud!**

CHAPTER FIVE
38. **Sympathy for the Devil**

CHAPTER SIX
44. **Respectable**

CHAPTER SEVEN
54. **It's only Rock'n'Roll (but I like it)**

63. *Albums*

64. *Index/Acknowledgments*

It is rare that a state-owned company receives any form of praise. Let it be at once stated, then, that it was courtesy of British Rail that the nucleus of the Rolling Stones, the formidable songwriting partnership of Jagger and Richards, was formed. Both have had their ups and downs, both are in need of some renovation, yet some 30 years later both British Rail and the Stones are now an indelible part of the British Establishment. The original rabble rousers, they raised two fingers to authority and a whole generation of teenagers

CHAPTER ONE
Please allow me to introduce myself

followed their lead. But their subsequent rise to fame soon transformed them into the darlings of the jet set.

In a railway carriage somewhere between London Bridge and Dartford was where the fateful meeting took place. They soon discovered their common interest was rhythm'n'blues – the 18-year-old Jagger was carrying a collection of American R&B albums, Richards his guitar. They found they had a mutual friend: Dick Taylor, at art college with Richards, was also playing with Mick in a band, Little Boy Blue and the Blue Boys. A shared passion for Chuck Berry sealed the friendship, and Richards was immediately recruited.

Richards was apparently not a motivated student. Undistinguished academically, he had left school for art college, where he continued not to distinguish himself save for a marked anti-authoritarian attitude. His parents, who were not wealthy, had bought him a guitar at the age of 15, and from that point in his life his energies were taken up with playing.

Jagger, by contrast, born into a comfortable middle class family, was encouraged academically, and, like a dutiful son, flourished. He was about to study politics and economics at the London School of Economics, the spawning ground of the political and economic intelligentsia. He nurtured the ambition of becoming an accountant, a tendency which was to stand him in good stead later in life.

In the days when British popular music was a distant and poor relation of the US brand, Jagger, Richards and Taylor set to work to learn much of the repertoire of American R&B artists Chuck Berry, Little Richard, Muddy Waters and the like. Regular trips to the Ealing Blues Club in west London provided the inspiration, and it was there that they first saw Brian Jones and Ian Stewart playing with Alexis Korner's Blues Incorporated. Alexis Korner was a seminal influence in the

development of the British R&B scene – the fluid line-up of Blues Incorporated included, over the years, such figures as Jack Bruce, Eric Clapton, Jeff Beck, Long John Baldry, Ginger Baker – the list is almost a Who's Who of British rock.

Jones had recently returned from a year touring Scandinavia, where he had gone to escape both the frustrations of life in Cheltenham and the young mothers of two illegitimate children. He was a bright if not precocious student and musician – he had learnt several instruments in his teens, including piano, clarinet, saxophone and guitar. He returned to London to seek out Korner, whom he had met on a visit to Cheltenham. He soon became a regular feature with the band. When Jagger and Richards saw Jones playing guitar, they recruited him to their ranks, and in turn began to play with Blues Incorporated themselves.

Another occasional member was drummer Charlie Watts, who had already declined to become a permanent fixture with Blues Incorporated, choosing instead to remain in his job as a commercial artist for an advertising agency. It was some time before he would give in to the other group members and join the Stones; he had a good job and wasn't about to throw his lot in with a bunch of long-haired misfits.

Their first appearance as the Rolling Stones came when Korner was invited to play for the BBC on Jazz Club, a popular radio program. The BBC, then as now strapped for cash, could only pay for six performers, and so only the main nucleus of Blues Incorporated could play. Jagger, Jones and Richards were among those left behind. Another problem was that Blues Incorporated were booked to play at the Marquee in Oxford Street on the same night. So Long John Baldry, Korner's support act, took over the spot at the Marquee and Jagger and the band were the support, christening themselves 'The Rollin' Stones,' the title taken from a Muddy Waters song, specially for the occasion. The line-up was: Mick Jagger (vocals); Brian Jones and Keith Richard (guitars); Ian Stewart (piano); Dick Taylor (bass) and Mick Avory (drums). This led to further bookings at the Marquee as well as the Ealing Jazz Club, and the band began to establish a loyal following.

Wyman was found next, via an ad following Dick Taylor's departure. According to Wyman, it was the fact that he owned his own amplifier that sealed his fate. They were a practical bunch even then. Brimming with expectation, they cut their first recordings. One of the tracks was entitled BRIGHT LIGHTS, BIG CITY. But they had to wait some time for both, as none of the record companies showed the slightest interest.

Above: **The Stones constantly acknowledged their debt to the black music scene and to artists such as Chuck Berry and Little Richard.**

Right: **The characteristic Stones pose. Jagger and Wyman look debonair, Jones stands a little apart. Meanwhile, Watts is clearly bemused and Richards is almost, but not quite, there.**

Previous page: **Their coats were brushed, their faces washed, their shoes were clean and neat. But they were soon to acquire a reputation for trouble, and it wouldn't be long before they abandoned the smiles. . .**

Above: **The Stones trying to find the tradesmen's entrance at Ivor Court.**

Left: **Notice of the Stones' first appearance at the Marquee on the wall of Bill Wyman's** Sticky Fingers **restaurant in London. Wyman is the group's historian, and the walls of the restaurant are covered with memorabilia from the Stones' 30-year career.**

One of the clubs the Stones regularly pestered for work was owned by Giorgio Gomelsky, a jazz fan who had helped Chris Barber organize jazz and blues festivals. Let down one time too many by his regular group, Gomelsky phoned Ian Stewart and the Stones began a residency at the club, which was in reality the back room of the Station Hotel, a pub in Richmond. They were soon packing the place out. It became one of the focal points for a movement which was slowly but surely edging jazz out in favor of R&B. Soon after,

CHAPTER TWO

You can't always get what you want

the club was named the Crawdaddy after the Bo Diddley number which the Stones often played at the end of their act on Sunday evenings. Eventually they were playing at the Crawdaddy four times a week. The Beatles came to hear them in April 1963, and George Harrison tried, unsuccessfully, to persuade Decca, the company who had earlier turned down the Beatles, to take them on.

It was Jones who contacted Andrew Oldham, a publicist who had just done some work for the Beatles, to try to persuade him to take a look at the band. When Oldham finally came along, he was astounded at what he saw. Probably the most significant element was audience reaction; Beatlemania had arrived, and everyone was looking for the new talent which would succeed them. Oldham felt he had found it in the seething mass of screaming fans at the Crawdaddy. Courtesy of Oldham the great Stones publicity machine got under way. Oldham planned to model them not along the lines of the Beatles, but in opposition to them. If the Beatles were the good guys, the Stones would be bad. The Beatles' hair was short and neat; their hair would be long and unkempt. Oldham's first rather brutal action as manager, though, was to dispense with Ian Stewart, who was told he did not fit the image Oldham had in mind. Stewart stayed on as road manager; he did not feel he could go back to his steady job at ICI now. Interestingly, none of the rest of the group even demurred.

Oldham's plausible patter secured them a contract with Decca, and he supervised their first recording session in May 1963. It should be pointed out, however, that Oldham's characteristic bluff had disguised the fact that he had absolutely no experience in recording whatever. The tapes were rejected by Decca, who insisted they were re-recorded

at their own studios. Released on 7 June 1963, their first single was the Chuck Berry song, COME ON, which had only been released in the US and was therefore little known in the UK. Entering the charts in July 1963, the group's first TV performance soon followed, when under Oldham's guidance, and characterized by the surly Jagger sneer, the group came across as arrogant and rebellious.

Wyman had to be persuaded to give up his job next; with a wife and child he was, like Watts, reluctant to risk his livelihood. But the most significant note of caution was sounded by Jagger himself; it was only after he had been assured that he could come back to complete his studies if things didn't work out with the band that he dropped his course at the LSE.

In September they began their first tour, supporting Bo Diddley. In deference to the great man they immediately cut all of the Bo Diddley numbers from their act. No doubt it was also considered prudent not to invite unfavorable comparisons. Ticket sales were poor, although the addition to the package of Little Richard, in the first week, helped to rescue the tour. However, it soon became evident that there was considerable tension between Jones and Jagger. The band discovered that Jones, who secretly considered himself to be the leader, had arranged to be paid an extra five pounds per week on this basis – a not inconsiderable sum at the time. As they began to make frequent TV appearances and attention was increasingly focused via the camera on Jagger, the situation could only get worse.

Looking for a follow up single to COME ON, the Stones had initially recorded a version of the Coasters' song, POISON IVY. Again the recording was supervised by Oldham, and again it was rejected by Decca. Jagger and Richards also attempted to compose something themselves, but this was similarly unsuccessful. At that time very few original songs were being composed by UK bands – only Lennon and McCartney had managed to break the US stranglehold, where black blues artists produced most of the hit tunes which were immediately covered by a suitably humbled UK scene.

Indeed it was due to a chance meeting between Oldham and Lennon and McCartney in the Piccadilly area of London that the Stones' second single came into being. The two Beatles had had an idea for a tune, and they accompanied Oldham to where the Stones were rehearsing. The song, I WANNA BE YOUR MAN, was finished there and then in front of the overawed group, and in two weeks the Stones had recorded it. Compared with the Beatles' own version it is

much more threatening; it may have been written by Lennon and McCartney, but the Stones had made the tune very much their own, and this illustrated perfectly the contrast between the two groups. A rather tired blues instrumental – their first original to be recorded, even if it was a decidedly unoriginal sound – was the B side. The single stayed for a while just outside the top ten, and the Stones were voted the sixth most popular UK group in the New Musical Express poll in 1963. But although Oldham continued to impress upon them the value of developing their own material, their further efforts were rather timid. A handful of compositions were recorded by other Decca artists, the most successful being Gene Pitney's THAT GIRL BELONGS TO YESTERDAY, which was the first of their songs to reach the top ten. But this, as well as other compositions, was noticeably imitative, and the strident and aggressive voice which was to become their trademark was hardly in evidence at this stage.

The next tour, early in 1964, was much more successful. Sharing the top of the bill with the Ronettes, the Phil Spector group who had just scored a big hit with the single BE MY BABY, they played to full houses nearly everywhere. By now the Stones desperately needed to release more material to sustain the public interest, but lacking the material to release an LP, they had to make do with an EP. Composed entirely of cover versions, many of which were rather unremarkable, it was popular mainly for one track, YOU BETTER MOVE ON, a number by Arthur Alexander, a US artist comparatively unknown in the UK. Other tracks included BYE BYE JOHNNY, another Chuck Berry number, and a version of MONEY, recently covered by the Beatles.

Another single, NOT FADE AWAY, an up-tempo version of the Buddy Holly song, followed in February. The B-side, LITTLE BY LITTLE, was composed in a few minutes in a corridor by Jagger and Phil Spector, who had arrived to help with recording. The single reached No. 3 in March. Touring as the record came out, they were this time topping the bill in their own right.

In April their first album was released. It included a Jagger-Richards composition, entitled TELL ME (YOU'RE COMING BACK). The remainder of the album consisted of cover versions, relying heavily on material penned by Chuck Berry, Bo Diddley, Muddy Waters and other black US artists. An interesting aspect of this release was the cover; there was no name or title, merely a photograph of the five Stones, taken by

Left and above: **An early appearance on** Ready, Steady, Go! *in 1963.*

Right: **The Stones relax over a cup of tea in 1964.**

Previous page: Jagger, Jones and Richards in the studio in 1964. To the left is Andrew Oldham, their manager. Second from right is Gene Pitney, the US artist who first took a Jagger/ Richards number, THAT GIRL BELONGS TO YESTERDAY, *into the top ten.*

Above: A slightly scruffier image of the Stones, circa 1964. Note Jagger's fringe, a sign of things to come. . .

Right and far right: **Further appearances on** Ready, Steady, Go!

Above right: **Richards and Watts relax with manager Andrew Oldham, who did his best to promote the Stones as a menacing alternative to the Beatles.**

the fashionable photographer David Bailey. The photo was in some ways a standard format, with the five group members side on to the camera. But the impression was unsettling, even hostile; the faces were half in shadow and this did nothing to hide the evident mute aggression in the pose. Soon the album was at No. 1.

A tour in May provoked more crowd trouble, and the police presence was strong. This can be partly attributed to the fact that more fans wanted to see the Stones than could possibly be accommodated in the venues, but it was equally true that Oldham was working hard to promote a bad-boy image for the group. As a commercial venture this exploitation of the generation gap proved highly successful. Much of the media coverage from this time on did not reveal the British Establishment in a very flattering light; paranoid and resistant to change as ever, the press began the popular pastime of Stone-baiting. Even the Melody Maker ran a story in March of that year headed WOULD YOU LET YOUR DAUGHTER GO WITH A ROLLING STONE? It has, however, been suggested that this may have been the handiwork of Oldham himself, quick as ever to realize the similarities between infamy and popularity, for commercial purposes at least.

The first of their US tours in June that year was a comparatively lukewarm affair by recent standards. Much less well known in the States, the reception was only really comparable in New York and Chicago, where they stopped off

to record an EP and the next single, a cover version of the Bobby Womack number, IT'S ALL OVER NOW, which was soon occupying the No. 1 slot in the UK. At the Chess studios, the pioneering label which had done so much to promote R&B, Muddy Waters, Willie Dixon and Chuck Berry called in to show their support. The EP contained another original composition, entitled EMPTY HEART.

Another trip to the States followed the release there of the album 12 × 5 in October. Reaction this time matched that of the UK tours, and the constant crowd trouble culminated in

a riot on the set of THE ED SULLIVAN SHOW. This national coverage was followed by expressions of disapproval from the mayors of Milwaukee and Cleveland among other public figures. More recording was done at the Chess studios, the environment which had recently produced such favorable results, and the single LITTLE RED ROOSTER soon reached No. 1 in the charts, backed with another original composition, OFF THE HOOK. Before they returned to the UK the cameras were there to record the Stones at the TAMI (Teen Age Music International) Show, where they topped a bill which included Chuck Berry, James Brown, the Supremes, the Beach Boys and Smokey Robinson. The film is still shown today, popularly known as GATHER NO MOSS.

The tour ensured that the album 12 × 5 lodged at No. 3 in the US charts for some time. HEART OF STONE was released in the US in January, and although it didn't reach the giddy heights of LITTLE RED ROOSTER, it was the first time an original composition was on the A side, and marked the rather unsteady beginning of a new phase for the Stones with the consolidation of the Jagger and Richards songwriting partnership. An Irish tour followed, where the audience expressed their support by throwing various missiles, among

them an iron bolt, a shoe and an ash tray – and those were just the ones that reached their targets, Jagger, Jones and Wyman respectively.

The UK version of the second album, entitled ROLLING STONES NO. 2, wasn't released until after Christmas, to avoid clashing with BEATLES FOR SALE, as was the custom in the years when the two groups vied for popularity. This imaginative title was not, however, even hinted at on the cover – like its

Left: *Richards makes a dash for the theater in Manchester, August 1964. Crowd control caused major problems for the police, and first aiders were kept busy as dozens of fans fainted in the crush before the group even appeared. . .*

Above: *Andrew Oldham in the studio in 1964. Although their contract stipulated he should produce their material, he had no previous experience, as the group soon discovered. On arriving in the studio he declared to the engineer: 'I don't know a damn thing about recording, or music for that matter.'*

predecessor, it consisted simply of a photograph of the band (once again by David Bailey) looking none too friendly in moody sinister semi-shade. But it was the back cover which was to provoke the outcry. Not content merely to hint at aggression, Oldham had supplied notes written in a pseudo streetwise slang largely of his own devising, which, when unraveled, much to Decca's surprise, suggested that anyone without the purchase price of the album would do well to mug a blind beggar or two in order to acquire the necessary funds. Decca reissued the record without the passage in question, but the damage was done.

The material itself was rather unremarkable. A couple of cover versions of Chuck Berry songs, another Muddy Waters song, a version of the Drifters' song UNDER THE BOARDWALK, and a few songs signaling a move towards more soul-based material were complemented by OFF THE HOOK, the B-side of LITTLE RED ROOSTER. Another two original compositions were included, but they seemed to lack the self-assurance which was to become their trademark in later years, showing that the Stones still had quite some way to go in their quest to topple the Beatles. Nevertheless, the album reached No. 1, and indeed stayed there for ten weeks, just a week short of the Beatles' recent achievement. How much of this was due to Oldham's inventive publicity campaign is a matter for speculation.

At the same time as recording the second album, the Stones had laid down two tracks which became their next single. Both Jagger-Richards compositions, THE LAST TIME and PLAY WITH FIRE shot to No. 1 as the group began their fifth UK tour. Security was tight, and attempts at crowd control appeared only to inflame the fans even more. Performances were almost inevitably curtailed, what music there was going unheard amid the screaming and shouting, and the group members, despite the security arrangements, had to be rescued from the engulfed stage minus much of their clothing. 'Three bars, and we'd be back in the hotel with a thousand quid,' according to Wyman. At the Manchester event, where a teenage girl fell from the dress circle, the Stones were all barred from the restaurant of the hotel in which they were staying because they weren't wearing ties, an event which was reported with great glee by the tabloids under the title 'The Rolling Stones Gather No Lunch.'

A European tour was followed by more dates in the US, where the Stones were working hard to sustain their popularity. A gig in California was the scene of an unfortunate incident when the band's getaway car was mobbed by fans. The Stones were trapped for some time and almost suffocated before the police waded in with batons flying to rescue them and, incidentally, inflict heavy casualties on the fans. UK dates that summer were followed by more hostile press coverage when Jagger, Jones and Wyman relieved themselves against the wall of a garage which had denied them – apparently quite arbitrarily – use of the toilet facilities. This was whipped up by the press to the point whereby charges were brought against the three for insulting behavior, an incident typical of the Establishment's attitude towards the Stones. No doubt it was fueled by the fact that they were in a chauffeur-driven Bentley at the time. To be scruffy and unwashed with long hair was not the British way, hardly the stuff on which the Empire was built. But to be all of those things and increasingly successful was clearly unbearable to many.

Right and bottom: **Jagger's increasingly energetic stage persona, late 1964.**

*T*he release of the next single in July 1965 was arguably the biggest step ever made in the progress of the group. It separated the earlier releases, derivative and often tentative, from the later work which is characterized mainly by an originality and maturity. (I CAN'T GET NO) SATISFACTION shot to No. 1 in the US a day after its release. In the UK it remained at No. 1 for three weeks. Even this achievement does not do the song justice; it is a classic track which in 1988 would be voted the best single of the last 25 years in a Rolling Stone survey. In

CHAPTER THREE

Satisfaction

the years since its release seldom a week has gone by without it receiving air play somewhere.

The album OUT OF OUR HEADS had already been released in the US, and had already been at the top of the charts for six weeks before it was released in the UK, with a different cover photo and also a largely different track listing. Mainly composed of cover versions, with just four original compositions, it was nevertheless a well-produced and polished recording in all senses. Yet it never made it to the top of the British charts. The reason was that the Beatles were still there with HELP!

This illustrated the central problem. The Beatles had begun their recording career in the same way as the Stones, recording cover versions of songs, largely by US artists, which they had popularized while playing clubs and the like. But the Beatles had long since abandoned this for albums entirely of their own material. OUT OF OUR HEADS was a good album, but it showed yet again that the Stones' move towards compositions of their own was overdue.

Even as the album was released, however, the Stones were putting this to rights, with a trip to the RCA studios on Sunset Boulevard especially to record material. It was during this trip that GET OFF OF MY CLOUD was recorded. The importance of this release cannot be overestimated; it was vital to release a single which would continue the momentum built up by SATISFACTION. It was another original composition, and its immediate success gave Jagger and Richards the confidence to approach the task of songwriting positively and without fear. And it had no trouble in reaching No. 1 on both sides of the Atlantic.

Shortly after the release of OUT OF OUR HEADS the Stones signed a new recording contract with Decca. They were

guaranteed three million dollars over the next five years, and Decca also agreed to make five million dollars available for a number of feature films, an area they were keen to pursue following the Beatles' successes in this line. The main reason for these greatly improved conditions was music publisher Allen Klein. Oldham had met with him to discuss publishing deals on the Stones' material, and Klein displayed such a forceful personality and shrewd understanding of business affairs that Oldham took him to meet Jagger and Richards. They agreed that he should become their co-manager, and it was due to his influence and force of character that the deal with Decca had been struck. The Stones were now on a far better royalty rate than the Beatles. This reflects in part the fact that the Beatles had not been so well advised at the start of their career – they had signed a five year deal when they were comparatively unknown and were still bound by it. Yet it also reflects that, due in no small part to Oldham's gifts as a publicist and the dangerous image the Stones courted, they were hot property, and probably doubly attractive to the ultra-conservative executives in the music business, with opposites attracting as always.

During the various tours which followed, Jagger and Richards were able to tackle songwriting with a new vitality and confidence. Most of the material for the next album was penned in various hotel bedrooms after shows. The UK tour was marked by the customary disturbances, although, strangely, each performance was concluded with the National Anthem. The tour in West Germany provoked the worst violence yet seen. From the beginning at Düsseldorf airport, where fans disrupted a press conference, to the concert there, the predominantly male following caused police enormous headaches. Andrew Oldham commented backstage that the audience reminded him of the Hitler Youth Movement; Jagger, in conciliatory mood as ever, responded by going on stage and goose-stepping and saluting to an audience that really needed no further incitement. Later that evening in the city 130 cars were wrecked and trains leaving for the suburbs were smashed. In West Berlin, the Hilton canceled their reservations, and a diplomatic incident began as West German fans wrecked East German trains.

Amid all the chaos Jagger and Richards nursed their injuries from various missiles and over-friendly crowds, and wrote the material that was to become AFTERMATH. It was recorded in December at the end of a US tour, ten new tracks recorded in just five days. The New Musical Express Poll Winners' Poll listed SATISFACTION as the best disk of the year,

Previous page: **Wyman takes center stage for this 1964 publicity shot but shies from the camera, left.**

Far left: **Inscrutable Keith, in the years before lines of excess became etched on his face.**

Left and above: **A comparatively cheerful group arrive at a concert, where (above) they receive armed protection from their devoted fans.**

and GET OFF OF MY CLOUD was third. The Stones were voted the best British R&B group, second-best British vocal group and second-best world vocal group. There are no prizes for guessing who came first in the last two categories.

The US tour was, of course, far better arranged under the auspices of Allen Klein; a private plane took them from one date to another and hotel accommodation was considerably more lavish. They were greeted in New York by a 100 foot illuminated picture of themselves in Times Square. Authority was more welcoming too; the governor of Denver declared the day after the show Rolling Stones Day, and following a concert in Boston the Stones were given the key to the city – and not just so they could let themselves out.

In June of that year Jagger, shortly after moving into his new home, collapsed from stress. His collapse was a fair measure of the pressure the Stones were under. In two weeks they were to start their fifth American tour.

At the start of the tour Oldham came up with another fine publicity stunt. When a number of New York hotels refused to accommodate the Stones, he announced that lawyers would be taking legal action over the unofficial ban. Of course, no such thing ever happened, but it gave the Stones a certain amount of advance publicity and brought their anti-authoritarian lifestyle and behavior to the fore at a time when the newspapers had begun to lose interest in their exploits.

Jagger's nervous exhaustion was typical of the experience of many groups who took on strenuous touring obligations and many public appearances (below), to ensure their continued success. Here Jagger relaxes at his new home near Regent's Park in London before another demanding tour (right).

All the Stones had recently bought lavish residences with the improved deals under Allen Klein's management. After Charlie Watts' purchase of a mansion in Sussex, his father, a truck driver, said: 'We are proud of Charlie, but we can't understand why he prefers an old place like this to something modern.'

Crowds in New York, Vancouver and Chicago among others prompted liberal (sic) use of batons and tear gas on the part of the police, and an incident in New York where an American flag was dragged across the floor nearly tipped the balance of unfavorable publicity against them, but Oldham was able to defuse the situation. Finally, in Honolulu, on 28 July, Jagger announced that the band were giving their very last performance.

The band took a well-earned break after the tour, each going his own separate way. In September, the new single, HAVE YOU SEEN YOUR MOTHER BABY, STANDING IN THE SHADOW was rather hesitantly received. It was a powerful but not immediately catchy number, probably characterized at the time as 'overambitious'. Energetic and possessing a very full sound, it needed a lot of listening to. Maybe staying out of the public gaze for so long had done them harm, with no concerts to promote interest in the release. Two other factors against it were the title (long titles, like long singles, were generally avoided) and the cover photo, which showed the five dressed as women. In their attempts to stay one step ahead in the outrage stakes, it seems that the Stones may have in some ways alienated their audience; transvestism was a difficult area. The film accompanying the release was banned by the UK chart show TOP OF THE POPS. Interestingly enough, however, after the original photo session in New York's Park Avenue the five wandered into a bar and ordered some beers.

Apparently nobody took the slightest notice. So when the photographer, Jerry Schatzberg, held a party for them after an appearance on the ED SULLIVAN SHOW, they turned up in Nazi uniforms. Quite a lot of people took notice on that occasion.

The end of the year saw Jagger break off his long-standing relationship with Chrissie Shrimpton, sister of model Jean, and replace her with Marianne Faithfull, the artist who had taken the Jagger/Richards song AS TEARS GO BY into the top ten back in 1964. Mick was going up in the world. Over Christmas a social clique had formed at Jones' flat in Courtfield Road, comprising Jones, Anita Pallenberg, Richards, Jagger, Marianne Faithfull and various celebrities, among whom were Tara Browne, antique dealer Christopher Gibbs and art gallery owner Robert Fraser.

The release of the next single, LET'S SPEND THE NIGHT TOGETHER, ruffled a few of the Establishment's feathers, but the BBC played the song without a murmur. In America,

though, various radio stations refused to play the song. And on the ED SULLIVAN SHOW Jagger can be seen mouthing 'let's spend some time together,' with obvious distaste. However, in an attempt to anticipate similar problems, it was released in the US with RUBY TUESDAY as the top side. The episode certainly was not of great importance, and indeed it is one of the few occasions when the powers-that-be showed themselves in a poor light without additional deliberate antagonism from the Stones and Oldham.

The release of BETWEEN THE BUTTONS followed later that month. It failed to come up to the standards set by AFTERMATH, and its chart progress reflects this. It appeared to be an ambitious attempt to broaden their range of writing styles, and it seems a shame, then, that for much of the time Jones was either laid out on the studio floor or absent; his versatility would have helped the end result. Much of the material is derivative and lacking in the bite characteristic of AFTERMATH. Another

reason for this could well be that the Stones had recorded and written much of the material under less pressurized conditions and had had more time to consciously attempt to extend their range, and of course the end of an arduous tour would not have been the most advisable time for such a task. AFTERMATH had been written following successes with SATISFACTION and GET OFF OF MY CLOUD and had been essentially a creative outpouring; BETWEEN THE BUTTONS came after HAVE YOU SEEN

Above: **Left to right are Flossie, Milly, Sara, Millicent and Penelope, seated, aka the Stones, posing for the cover photo of** HAVE YOU SEEN YOUR MOTHER, BABY, STANDING IN THE SHADOW *in New York's Central Park.*

Above right: **Jones playing autoharp on** Ready, Steady, Go! *in late 1966.*

Right: **This time it's Jones' turn to forget the chords. The Stones on the set of the Ed Sullivan Show, July 1966.**

YOUR MOTHER and suffered from being rather too premeditated. Nevertheless, BACK STREET GIRL is an excellent example of spontaneous vitriol, one of the nastiest and most misogynist songs even Jagger has ever written.

When first approached in April 1965 the Stones had refused to appear on SUNDAY NIGHT AT THE LONDON PALLADIUM, a televized variety show, because it did not suit their image. This despite the fact that its audience figures were colossal, and the nationwide exposure would have been very valuable. A quintessentially family show, it closed each week with a host of family entertainers waving goodbye to viewers and audience from a revolving carousel. In January 1967 the Stones finally agreed to take part. However, at the end of the show, viewers looked in vain for their friendly smiling faces on the carousel. This caused no small stir among the nation as a whole. Ironically, those most incensed at the Stones' non-appearance were almost certainly those who resented their presence in any case. But the show was as much a part of British Sunday family life as church, something which Jagger doubtless understood from comments after the resultant furore: 'That carousel thing isn't an altar, it's just a drag'. The mistake, of course, had been appearing in the first place; one can hardly imagine the Stones taking part in such a ritual and retaining any credibility. But more than any other action it stored up resentment against them which would spill over during the following year.

*1*967 was the year of flower power. To those at the periphery of the movement, whose contact with events was through the newspapers, this was largely characterized by two things: sex and drugs. Even rock'n'roll was relegated to a poor third that year. One of the most lurid drug exposés appeared in the down-market News of the World on 5 February. It went into great detail in exposing the groups which made use of various drugs, and among them the favorite bêtes noires, the Stones, naturally found a prominent place.

CHAPTER FOUR

Get off of my cloud!

Mick Jagger was quoted extensively. And also mistakenly. Many of the comments were in fact made by Brian Jones and not Jagger, and were in any case made almost a year previously. Jagger's solicitors issued a libel writ, and the newspaper, which did not recognize such fine distinctions in its fearless quest to uncover the truth, responded aggressively. Largely, this was a result of their recognizing their own mistake; damages were likely to be substantial. And so it was that private detectives were hired by the paper to tail Jagger and Richards. The following Sunday the police were informed of various illicit goings-on at Redlands, Richards' home in Sussex, and when the police arrived the newspaper was already there to record the event, which duly appeared in the next edition.

The newspaper finally felt it had found justification for its allegations. Jagger, Richards and Robert Fraser were charged under the Dangerous Drugs Act, although many of the other guests were in possession of larger quantities of drugs and more incriminating substances. Acid had been taken by most of the members of the party throughout the day. However, the police were clearly only interested in Jagger and Richards. Indeed, Jagger had previously been warned that the police were out to get him. It seems hard to avoid concluding that the whole business was a set-up.

While various chemicals were being analyzed, they decided to get out of the country, and made for Tangier, in Morocco. Jones was soon hospitalized with a bad asthma attack, and Richards and Anita Pallenberg began increasingly to enjoy each other's company, much to Jones' distress when he rejoined the group. Eventually relationships deteriorated to the point whereby Jones was left behind by the others without even a note, while he was out recording ethnic tribal music.

A three-week tour of the continent was in the offing, a comparatively relaxed affair, and the only one planned that year. In the event, it was a highly-charged business, ruined by personal tensions and the worries of the forthcoming trial, as well as repeated and protracted humiliating searches by customs at every turn. The crowd trouble persisted throughout. In Sweden, dogs were used when fans threw fireworks on to the stage along with the more usual bits of seating and bottles. In Vienna the crowd preferred a smoke bomb to express its approval and in Paris trouble developed into a full-scale riot between police and fans in the street outside the theater. In Warsaw trouble began when 12,000 fans were denied tickets. Apparently party officials had monopolized ticket distribution and armored cars and water hoses had to be used to control an angry mob. The last concert in Zurich saw repeat performances by the crowd there.

On his return Jagger was charged with possession of pep pills, bought legally in Italy but prohibited in Britain unless obtained on prescription, and Richards was charged with allowing his house to be used for smoking cannabis. On the day they were granted bail Jones was arrested and charged with possession of Indian hemp. Richards left the country to spend the time until their trial with Anita Pallenberg, who was in Rome working on Roger Vadim's BARBARELLA with Jane Fonda. He returned only for recording sessions and to arrange matters pertaining to the trial. The Stones were later to explain how the pressure of the forthcoming trial had disrupted the group's work throughout this period.

At the trial, Judge Block made much of the prosecution's evidence stating that Marianne Faithfull (known only as Miss X, despite the fact that the whole country was well aware of her identity) had been found naked at the time of the arrest. Apparently she had been wrapped in a rug, and was the only woman present at the occasion. The suggestion of group sex with a convent-educated girl struck at the very heart of the values the News of the World supposedly held dear, and this was salaciously reported in minute detail in its pages for its readers to salivate over. Much was made of her former innocence and purity and her subsequent decline into depravity and corruption at the hands of the bad boys of rock'n'roll. What the judge had omitted to mention was that such behavior was not illegal in itself. All three, however, were found guilty. Jagger was sentenced to three months, Fraser to six and Richards to twelve months imprisonment.

The severity of the sentence brought widespread criticism from the country at large. Fans protested outside the

offices of the News of the World, *and The Who issued a recording of* UNDER MY THUMB *and* THE LAST TIME, *donating their profits to the defense costs of the group. The most significant support, however, came from* The Times. *William Rees-Mogg, the editor, contributed an editorial demonstrating that Jagger and Richards had been made examples of and had been denied normal British justice. Pointing out that Richards had been convicted on purely circumstantial evidence and that Jagger had unwittingly committed an offense which was of a purely technical nature, the editorial had great influence on the subsequent appeal. The Appeal Court ruled that Judge Block had misdirected the jury and had allowed them to be swayed by the behavior of Miss X; as a result Richards' conviction was quashed. Jagger's was allowed to stand, but he was given a conditional discharge. Sadly, Fraser had to serve his six-month sentence for possession of heroin.*

Meanwhile Jones was increasingly suffering under the strain of his forthcoming trial. He took little part in recording, and on 6 July was taken into hospital suffering from stress. On 30 October he pleaded guilty to the charge of possession and was sentenced to nine months, another excessively severe sentence. The Establishment was not beaten yet.

*Previous page: **The Stones relax on a park bench while the authorities begin a concerted effort to make an example of them to the nation's young. The Stones' image as self-proclaimed role models for the young and angry, made them the conservative establishment's No. 1 enemy as the summer of love got under way.***

*Left: **Jagger, Jones and Richards arriving at Zurich, April 1967.***

*Below left: **Marianne Faithfull with Jagger earlier that year.***

*Right: **Jagger and Richards leaving Chichester Magistrates Court, Christmas 1967, after being charged with possession.***

*Below: **An enthusiastic fan makes contact with Jagger at London's Royal Albert Hall.***

Brian Jones (above right, and left): 'Our generation is growing up with us and they believe in the same things we do. Nearly all of them think like us and are questioning some of the basic immoralities which are tolerated in present day society; the war in Vietnam, persecution of homosexuals, illegality of abortion, drug taking. All of these things are immoral. We are making our own statement, others are making more intellectual ones. We believe there can be no evolution without revolution. I realize there are other inequalities; the ratio between affluence and reward for work done is all wrong. I know I earn too much, but I'm still young and there's something spiteful inside me which makes me want to hold on to what I've got.'

Right: In 1967 the Stones were no more immune to flower power than any other group. Jagger and Marianne Faithfull even joined the Beatles on their pilgrimage to the Maharishi Mahesh Yogi in Bangor, North Wales.

Unfortunately, however, a significant own goal was scored by Judge Block again, at the Horsham Ploughing and Agricultural Society dinner, of all unlikely places. In an after-dinner speech he allowed his discourse, loosely based on farming, to drift on to the subject of stones, attesting that he had tried his best to cut certain 'stones' down to size, sadly to no avail, as the Appeal Court had 'let them roll free'. With Jones' appeal still to be heard, the remarks were clearly *sub judice*. This, together with a suitably repentant speech by Jones at the appeal and evidence from three psychiatrists who attested to Jones' mental strain at the time of the offense ensured that the original sentence was set aside.

In September the five group members met with Allen Klein, ostensibly for 'business talks'. However, the purpose of the meeting soon became clear when the Stones' press office announced that the partnership between them and Oldham had been dissolved. During recording sessions that summer they had sat around playing standard blues riffs rather badly until he left. The row backstage at the London Palladium may have been one cause for the estrangement, as Oldham had tried to make them join the show's finale. It has also been suggested that he may have been blamed for the lack of success of the last album, BETWEEN THE BUTTONS, although

such an attitude would be hard to justify. But maybe the most significant reason was that with more than their fair share of notoriety recently they felt they no longer needed Oldham's gift for attracting bad publicity.

Work on the forthcoming album, THEIR SATANIC MAJESTIES REQUEST, had of course been constantly interrupted throughout the preceding year. Indeed it was remarkable that any creative work was done under such conditions, especially considering the reception accorded to the last album. Another factor would almost certainly have been the release of the Beatles' SERGEANT PEPPER'S LONELY HEARTS CLUB BAND. Apparently Brian Wilson, of the Beach Boys, had been so

overawed by the quality of the album on hearing it that he had abandoned the music he was working on. Jagger himself had been immeasurably impressed by the work, but had chosen instead to try to match it. The results were variable. Like the last album, it lacked the hard edge and purpose of AFTERMATH, although some of the attempts to broaden their songwriting range were successful, such as 2000 LIGHT YEARS FROM HOME and SHE'S A RAINBOW, both of which were included on the second compilation album, THROUGH THE PAST DARKLY. In terms of emulating the SERGEANT PEPPER album it was clearly not a success, however. Maybe the primary problem in this respect was the cover, which was such an obvious imitation of the SERGEANT PEPPER cover as to be bordering on pastiche.

The Stones had always resisted the charge that they took their inspiration from the Beatles, yet here they were quite clearly (and rather unsuccessfully) following their lead. The public reception was poor, and so commercially as well as musically the album was unsuccessful, although one interesting feature is that it contained a track written by Bill Wyman, IN ANOTHER LAND, released as a single later that year.

The poor reception given to THEIR SATANIC MAJESTIES REQUEST was the cue for the Stones to make a determined effort to bounce back. They decided to abandon the avant-garde flavor of this last album and move back to R&B. Then they contacted a producer. It seemed that their own enthusiasm for the possibilities offered by the modern studio had brought out the worst in them, and they felt the need for some guidance. This arrived in the form of Jimmy Miller, an independent producer who had worked recently with the Spencer Davis Group, and whose work was widely admired. Jagger, Richards and Miller worked on songs for the album throughout the first part of 1968.

The album was taking longer than envisaged and so in May of that year they issued a single in advance which announced their intention of getting back to R&B based material and showed a new purposeful and insistent Stones. The song was JUMPIN' JACK FLASH. They previewed the song at the 1968 NME Pollwinners' Concert, where they played it and

SATISFACTION to rapturous applause. The promotional video for the song shows Jagger at his best, injecting the performance with a raw energy which signaled the rebuilding of their reputation. The song quickly topped the charts worldwide.

In September Jones was found guilty of possession of cannabis. This was his second offence and, although the original sentence had been set aside, the Stones feared that he would receive a lengthy prison term. But the case was heard at the Inner London sessions where magistrates were more enlightened, and Jones was fined £50 with £150 costs. Despite this it was envisaged that his two convictions would be a problem were the band to attempt a tour. Shortly

*Left: **The Stones had always been keen to distance themselves from any particular movement; Jagger was a shrewd enough businessman to realize that if they became too closely identified with a particular trend, they would just as surely die with it. THEIR SATANIC MAJESTIES REQUEST was their only venture into psychedelia and the concept was highly derivative.***

*Right: **Keith Richards accompanies Anita Pallenberg in 1967. Her estrangement from Jones and her relationship with Richards caused tension in the group at a time when the Stones were struggling for a new direction.***

Above: **Live footage of the Stones developing and recording the track** SYMPATHY FOR THE DEVIL, **the opening track on the next album,** BEGGAR'S BANQUET. **Film of this was used extensively in the Jean-Luc Godard movie** One Plus One, *a fascinating* *record of the Stones' working methods. It also reveals a very subdued Jones (left).*

Right: **A view of the Stones in laid-back mood (top) and a still (below) from the TV spectacular,** Rock 'n' Roll Circus.

afterwards, Jones purchased Cotchford Farm in Sussex, where AA Milne had written Winnie-the-Pooh.

In December BEGGAR'S BANQUET was finally released. In the meantime a single taken from the album had been released in the US, STREET FIGHTIN' MAN, written in celebration of the student riots in Paris that summer and banned by the majority of states for that reason. Strangely, Decca had released the single in a cover which consisted of a photograph of rioting in Los Angeles that year, although whether out of malice or ineptitude one can only guess. The single did very badly, although it is a very powerful and impressive song, opening side two of the album. Much of the album was directly drawn from the Stones' background in blues, and while it could only reach No. 2 in the US and No. 3 in the UK, it nevertheless reaffirmed the Stones' pre-eminence in the music world.

It was not until the spring months of 1969 that the group reassembled. A lot of the material for the next album had been recorded prior to the belated release of BEGGAR'S BANQUET, but a few tracks were still needed. As the work was nearing completion Jagger and Marianne Faithfull were arrested at their flat in Cheyne Walk, Chelsea, and charged with possession of cannabis resin. It was the first in a series of events which were to mark the year as a turning point in the Stones' development.

CHAPTER FIVE

Sympathy for the Devil

For some time the other Stones had been aware that Brian Jones had become a liability. He was frequently absent from recording sessions, suffered from stress or drug-related illness on tour, and both his heavy use of drugs and his resultant convictions made it difficult for the Stones to continue to see him as a part of the team, although Richards especially would soon amass a much more impressive list of convictions himself.

Jagger and Richards went to see him on 8 June, with Charlie Watts to lend moral support, and confronted him. The upshot of the meeting was Jones' announcement that 'the Stones' music is not to my taste any more. I want to play my own kind of music.' Initially it seemed a positive move for both sides. Jones talked enthusiastically of writing his own material, and early in 1967 had written the soundtrack for a film, A DEGREE OF MURDER, by the German director Volker Schlöndorff and starring Anita Pallenberg, although he had not contributed to any of the studio albums. The Stones were able to announce an immediate replacement in the form of Mick Taylor, formerly of John Mayall's Bluesbreakers. He was little known, but Richards had professed great admiration for his playing. His live debut with the band was to be at a free concert in Hyde Park on 5 July, less than a month away.

The next turbulent event of that year took place two days before the concert. Jones, who had been taking sleeping pills and had earlier been drinking brandy, was found face down in his swimming pool. It appeared that the drink and tablets had simply sent him to sleep, and he had drowned very suddenly. In all probability the whole episode was a complete accident, although speculation on the part of the media was rife. In the event the Stones decided it was best to go ahead with the concert as arranged. They dedicated it to Brian,

declaring at the start of the show that 'Brian would have wanted it to go on. I hope people will understand that it is because of our love for him that we are still doing it.' Jagger began the concert by reading a poem by Shelley and releasing butterflies into the crowd of around 300,000.

The day before the concert the Stones had released a single which was to continue the drive developed by JUMPIN' JACK FLASH. It was HONKY TONK WOMEN, and reached No. 1 later that month. On the B-side was the contrasting YOU CAN'T ALWAYS GET WHAT YOU WANT, featuring the London Bach Choir. Just as the summer came to an end, the second greatest hits album, THROUGH THE PAST DARKLY, was released. It was an apt title to follow what had been an eventful season. But it was not over yet; the darkest episode was yet to come.

In November the Stones began their American tour. All tickets were sold within hours, despite arrangements for a fourth concert at the Madison Square Gardens and another at the Los Angeles Forum. In response to complaints that ticket prices were too high, the Stones arranged a free open air concert in San Francisco along the lines of the one in Hyde Park, to thank their fans. In the event the concert was attended by over half a million people, and traffic jams built up around Altamont, in Livermore, California, for 20 miles in all directions. The Stones, however, arrived by helicopter. Support acts included Santana, Jefferson Airplane and Crosby, Stills, Nash and Young. Crowd control was obviously going to be a problem, although the audience hysteria had not been as pronouced as on their most recent visit, and so it was that Jerry Garcia of the Grateful Dead suggested the local chapter of Hell's Angels as security.

This may seem an ill-fated decision in retrospect, but to be fair on the Stones the security at Hyde Park had been provided by Hell's Angels, and the Stones felt rightly or wrongly that the police had hardly distinguished themselves on previous occasions; after all, injuries had been disturbingly high over the years and batons had been wielded on many occasions with more or less disastrous results. Also the Grateful Dead had considerable experience in organizing precisely this kind of event, and the one thing nobody could have predicted was the size of the crowd and the special problems of maintaining order that would bring. Events that day certainly seem to have taken everyone by surprise. One thing that should have been no surprise, many felt after the event, was the way in which the Hell's Angels panicked and over-reacted. They were over-zealous if not positively brutal in suppressing the more lively elements of the crowd, acting in

Previous page: **Jagger in** Sympathy For The Devil. *The satanic pose would later catch up with the group.*

Right: **Jagger and Marianne Faithfull arriving in London to face charges of possessing marijuana, May 1969.**

Far right: **Brian Jones' funeral, Cheltenham, 10 July 1969. Jones' mother and father follow immediately behind the coffin.**

just the way that Jagger had accused the police of behaving. Several people were beaten quite badly with pool cues, and a number were injured when one Angel rode his bike into the crowd near the stage. Overall at least 20 serious injuries were recorded. The most notorious and tragic incident, however, was captured on film by David and Albert Maysles, who were at the event to record live footage of the Stones. The film can still be seen today under the title of GIMME SHELTER.

During the afternoon Marty Balin of Jefferson Airplane,

Left and below: **The Stones at the free concert in Hyde Park in the summer of 1969. Despite Brian Jones' death just two days earlier, it was felt that the show should go on. It was dedicated to Jones, and marked the first public appearance of Mick Taylor, Jones' replacement.**

one of the support groups, had been involved with, and indeed injured by, the Hell's Angels when he had interceded in a disturbance with some of the fans, and the mood was already distinctly nasty. The Stones first took the stage at 11 pm, some four hours late, and tensions were running high. It was as Jagger was singing SYMPATHY FOR THE DEVIL that a young black man, Meredith Hunter, attempted to get up on to the stage. The Angels beat him back and then stabbed him to death in full view of the group. They later claimed that he had pulled a gun, although no weapon was ever found. Richards reacted to the event to some extent, but Jagger, who later insisted he did not see what was taking place, simply continued, if a little shaken. It was only from the following day's newspapers that most people knew of the event.

Newspaper coverage could hardly fail to hold the Stones responsible. Some of the reports made much of the satanic imagery; sympathy for the devil, the 'satanic majesties', Jumpin' Jack Flash, and the fact that the security had been provided by Hell's Angels. Also at that time the track MIDNIGHT RAMBLER was being released. It was based on the exploits of the Boston Strangler, and was heavy with danger and brooding evil which, although recorded before Altamont, was damning in retrospect. It appeared on the album LET IT BLEED, a worthy successor to BEGGAR'S BANQUET in every way, as it is in the same blues-inspired vein as the former, but expands style and subject matter without wandering into the excesses of THEIR SATANIC MAJESTIES. Ironically, the title of the album was used by festival promoter Rock Scully in a comment after the event on the incident: 'The Rolling Stones signed the contract. They've got what they paid for. Let it bleed, man!' And it seemed that to some extent this was true, as the Angels had been paid for their work in beer. But whatever the rights and wrongs, the Stones seemed to have made a mistake in trying to avoid any personal responsibility for the events that day. Seen alongside Jagger's egoistic cavorting on stage, the stabbing of a fan while they played on regardless did not look good. It was with some justification that Rolling Stone reported: 'Altamont was the result of diabolic egoism and, most of all, a lack, a fundamental lack, of humanity.' Even they couldn't resist the suggestion of diabolism, but the message is surely justified.

The Stones returned to Britain to play two dates in London amid all the publicity that Altamont had engendered.

Left: **No, it's not Michael Jackson. The lead singer of the Rolling Stones in one of his off-the-shoulder numbers.**

Above right: **Richards and Jagger in a climactic scene from Gimme Shelter, the film of the tour which ended at Altamont.**

Right: **The Maysles brothers' cameras are there to capture events in the film Gimme Shelter, including the violent crowd scenes which would later end in tragedy.**

Throughout the year the Stones had been looking around the south of France with a view to buying property. Richards was ostensibly trying to find a way round Anita Pallenberg's problems with immigration officials, who had insisted that she could only remain in the country if they married, a step they were both reluctant to take. Jagger had good reason to feel less at home in the UK than he might, for all the Stones had to some extent been plagued by the media, and Jagger and Richards had continually been made

CHAPTER SIX

Respectable

examples of by the authorities. Looking around, they liked what they saw. All five bought lavish residences in the south of France and in March 1971 announced they would be going into tax exile.

There can be little doubt that this was widely seen as a major snub to their fans. Their rebellious anti-authoritarian stance fitted ill beside such a move, identifying them with the excessively rich, and setting them apart from their fans. Moreover, they set a precedent in this too, for many other top names were to follow them in the years that followed. It also came at a time when they had dispensed with Klein and were beginning to amass even more money by taking control of their own careers; the recent North American tour had grossed a record $2 million. However, shortly after this decision Jagger was again the victim of a raid, with photographers already at the scene waiting for the police to arrive. It was a clumsy maneuver and charges were not pressed, but it served to remind Jagger of the joys he was leaving behind.

A farewell tour early in March prompted thousands across the UK to queue for tickets for whole days. Shortly afterwards they left for Richards' home and their mobile studio on the coast between Nice and Monte Carlo at Villefranche-sur-Mer. As STICKY FINGERS was released, on their own label within Atlantic Records with the famous tongue logo designed by Andy Warhol, they were recording material for the next release. The album itself was musically in the tradition established by BEGGAR'S BANQUET and LET IT BLEED, although there are fewer statements of social rebellion than previously, beginning the move towards songs more in the conventional rock'n'roll mold. Heavily laden with drug references, it is rebellious in a more personal way perhaps. After Altamont and the tumultuous events of 1969 this was to become the norm;

the Stones were no longer to be the anarchic influence they once were. Instead they took on the mantle of 'the world's greatest rock'n'roll band', a much more lucrative position, although significantly this was only possible with the break-up of their long-time rivals the Beatles.

The recording sessions for EXILE ON MAIN STREET, a double album, were also significant in that Jagger, who had only recently married Bianca Perez Moreno de Macias, would frequently dash off to be with her in Paris, where she was pregnant. Richards was increasingly left in charge, and his influence is heard in the country flavor of much of the album. Soon Richards was to start a period of heavy involvement with drugs, while Jagger courted the jet set with Bianca. Mick would gradually take charge of the group's financial affairs, an area in which Richards was less willing to involve himself. It seemed that Jagger was about to realize his teenage dream of being an accountant. But the differences which began to appear between the two were to cause the band major problems almost leading to their break-up on repeated occasions.

In marrying Bianca, Mick Jagger had forged a direct link with a large part of the social élite. The two of them became the staple diet of the gossip columnists and society pages. They began to move in chic circles in New York, both featuring prominently (and very unflatteringly) in the Andy Warhol diaries, for example. Meanwhile Richards became more estranged and more openly contemptuous of his lifestyle. Jagger, moreover, had cleaned up his image after 1969 and was to become increasingly intolerant of the effect of drugs on Richards. The greatest casualty of the breakdown of their professional and personal relationship was, of course, the music.

The album EXILE ON MAIN STREET soon reached No. 1 on its much anticipated release in May 1972, although it fell back very quickly afterwards. An album of uniformly high quality, it nevertheless had no obvious singles or outstanding tracks to immediately capture attention. Today it is regarded as a classic album, but at the time it marked if anything a lull in the band's popularity. It certainly took more listening to than recent releases, and was more difficult to assimilate simply because there was twice as much to take in. But the intervening years have only increased its popularity and importance in the Stones catalog.

Shortly after the release the Stones commenced their seventh North American tour. Described by the tour organizer, Peter Rudge, as 'not like a rock'n'roll tour, more like the Normandy landing', it began inauspiciously when all except dependable Bill Wyman missed the flight. The tour itself set a

precedent which other bands were to try and live up to; with the Stones in financial control the whole affair was incredibly lavish, with a retinue of cooks, chauffeurs and roadies in constant attendance. For the first time concerts were promoted with T-shirts and other merchandise, and the great rock'n'roll circus was born. The Chicago Sunday Times *wrote:* 'They were famous; now they are a legend.' If so, this was to a great extent, a legend of their own making. The spectacle was the thing, and the music was beginning to take second place.

Crowd trouble was minimal; audiences were older and more respectful now, and there was less unfavorable media coverage. The tour of 1972 marked a definite change in the way the Stones functioned as a group. During the following years other tours followed the same pattern, and the legend was further strengthened; this was the age when the tour was an event in itself, with its T-shirts, hot dog stalls and vast panoply of merchandise. The lavishness was matched only by the amount grossed on each subsequent occasion. More than this, though, Jagger's growing social whirl with the jet set left the Stones living their lives quite separately, meeting only for recording sessions and tours which by now were as infrequent

Previous page: **Keith Richards trying very hard to look respectable and Bill Wyman (above) looking very glamorous.**

Above left: **Keith and Anita, proud parents of Marlon, 1969.**

Left: **An early promotional picture for the launch of their own label, Rolling Stones Records.**

Above: **Jagger in fine voice on his wedding day, serenading bride Bianca Perez Morena de Macias.**

as they were lavish.

The album which followed EXILE ON MAIN STREET was GOAT'S HEAD SOUP. Released in 1973, it was preceded by a single, the slow ballad ANGIE. The single did extremely well, but when the album came out the disappointment was all the greater for it. In attempting to broaden their range they had lost a little of the characteristic hard edge again. And of course after Altamont the album no longer had as much material calculated to shock, always a useful tool in stimulating public interest. The contentious STAR, STAR was a song about groupies which Jagger had, on Atlantic's insistence, been forced to change from the original title STARFUCKER.

The following year saw the release of another disappointing album. IT'S ONLY ROCK'N'ROLL contained some interesting tracks, such as the slow TIME WAITS FOR NO-ONE, but it seemed, ironically, that this was another album which did little more than mark time for the Stones. The title track was released as a single, only reaching No. 10 in the UK and No. 18 in the US. There are certainly better tracks on the album. The tune is very repetitious, indeed it might be said that it consists largely of one line repeated more or less ad infinitum, at most a single idea. Another problem is the subject matter. It parodies the outrageous behavior of rock groups, although

Right: **Ron Wood was drafted in to replace Mick Taylor, who announced his departure late in 1974. His flamboyant stage presence and his sense of humor meant that he soon became a permanent fixture with the band.**

Below: **Jagger and David Bowie in 1973. Over ten years later they would team up on a video as part of the Live Aid project.**

Above: **Probably the biggest fashion mistake in the world. The Stones plumb depths other bands cannot reach in their quest to move with the times.**

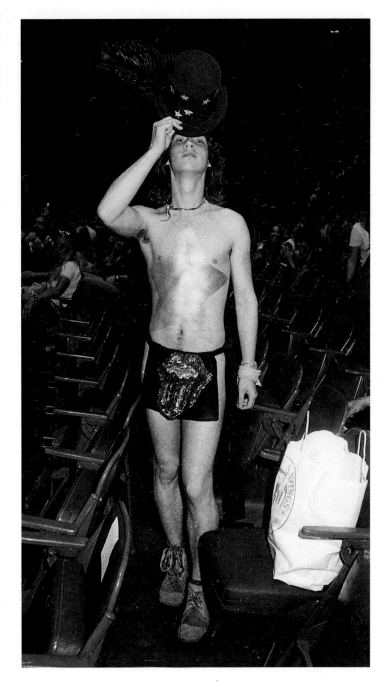

the race, fitted the group's image so well that he immediately slotted in. At first it was announced that he would be guesting on the forthcoming 1975 tour of America, as Jagger, publicly at least, insisted that nothing should be done to compromise the Faces' line up. But then Rod Stewart declared that he was quitting the Faces to go solo. Ron Wood was in. The next album shows him on the cover although he was only one of three additional guitarists featured.

The 1975 tour was if anything more extravagant. The stage itself was shaped into a lotus flower, and when the whole thing opened out it revealed a Stone at each of the five petals. Also featured was a 20 foot inflated phallus which Jagger made much of during performance; further delusions of grandeur no doubt. Those in the front seats were showered with buckets of water during some performances. In short, the

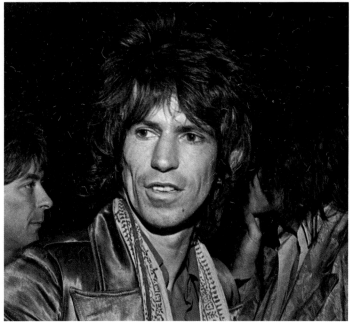

some might say the Stones were the most guilty of excess themselves. In retrospect it certainly seems that the Stones were grotesquely parodying themselves, even if they didn't realize this at the time.

When the Stones met to put together the next album it was without Taylor. He announced he would be pursuing his own work. It came as quite a shock, as although he was essentially too shy to fit in with the Stones' persona, his contributions to the albums in terms of musicianship were considerable, and the albums he appeared on were among the Stones' best. Rumors immediately circulated as to his most likely replacement. Wayne Perkins was favorite for a time. Also in the running were Jeff Beck, Steve Marriott, Mick Ronson and Rory Gallagher.

In the event the new album, BLACK AND BLUE, featured three guitarists in addition to Richards; Perkins, Harvey Mandel and Ron Wood, then with the Faces. Wood, a late entrant into

tour was designed with excess in mind, with the aim of out-doing anything that had gone before. It was outrageous, but really rather pointless; excess essentially for its own sake.

BLACK AND BLUE showed an attempt to assimilate various different sounds, among them salsa and urban New York funk, with a rather lukewarm result. The direct lifting of a reggae song, Eric Donaldson's CHERRY OH BABY, was distinctly unsuccessful. Yet again, a slow number was released as a single and did reasonably well. FOOL TO CRY was a good example of the slower material the Stones were beginning to develop successfully, in contrast to their derivative attempts to move with the times. Only one more album remained now for the contract with Atlantic to be at an end. They planned to make it a live double album, and as Wood and Richards sifted live material Jagger began to publicly announce conditions for the signing of a new agreement, including huge advances. Jagger acknowledged that the signing of the Stones would be

Left: *Jagger looking a little ruffled in mid-1976 as the band begins to lose direction.*

Below: *Mick and Keith relax backstage during a concert tour of Australia.*

Above: *Ron 'n' Keef again. In Wood, Richards had found a kindred spirit, and on and off stage their personalities sparked each other off. The album SOME GIRLS, on which his contribution is first really felt, got them back on the rails again and outsold all their previous albums to date.*

a matter of prestige; he didn't expect any company to make money from their catalog.

The Stones had decided to record some fresh material for the forthcoming live album, and it was while in Toronto, recording classics such as Chuck Berry's AROUND AND AROUND and LITTLE RED ROOSTER in a small club atmosphere, that Richards was busted by the Mounted Police. Such a large quantity of heroin was discovered that he was charged with the much more serious offense of trafficking, for which a long sentence could have been imposed. Media interest was revived when Richards acknowledged he had become addicted in the mid-seventies, taking the drug to combat boredom and depression after long tours, and articles began to appear detailing the process. An impending cocaine trial in the UK was completely overshadowed by the possibility of a life sentence at the Canadian trial, and it was acknowledged by the group as a real threat to their future. In the event,

however, Richards and Pallenberg committed themselves to a hospital to overcome their addiction, and Richards was only fined and ordered to play two charity concerts for the blind when the case was eventually heard in October 1978.

With the signing of a new deal, bigger and better publicity was at hand for the Stones. The next album, SOME GIRLS, released in 1978 was their biggest selling album ever. More than anything, though, they seem to have gained a fresh impetus, partly due, no doubt, to the influence of Ron Wood. For the first time since late 1974 they were able to get together as a complete five-man unit. Ron Wood had been playing with the Stones since early 1975, and when the album appeared it was evident that the combination had meshed. Richards was off heroin at last, his cure providing inspiration for the song BEFORE THEY MAKE ME RUN, on which Richards takes lead vocal. It seemed that they were ready to consolidate their reputation as serious musicians again after the uncertainties

Left: Ron Wood was increasingly credited with compositions alongside Jagger and Richards on the albums which followed SOME GIRLS. His outgoing character meshed well with the Stones' outlandish behavior both on and off stage.

Right: A publicity shot for the Stones' Tour of the Americas, 1975. Left to right: Ron Wood, Billy Preston, Ollie Brown, Jagger and Richards.

and excesses of the previous few years. The album contained much fresh material, and innovative songs such as MISS YOU, released as a single in advance of the album, with its contemporary disco rhythm, and the tongue-in-cheek FAR AWAY EYES, which doffs its cap to country. These both worked well in their own right, rather than existing merely as slavish imitations with no original merit. With a few hard-driving tracks based on solid and catchy riffs as well, the album was a must for all rock fans by the middle of 1978.

The album made No. 1 in the States halfway through the North American tour of that year. The excesses of the previous tour were largely absent, and the Stones took in a few smaller venues. Meanwhile, some of the lyrics on the album were causing problems in the States. Jesse Jackson, head of Operation PUSH (People United to Save Humanity) threatened pickets and boycotts after denouncing the lyrics of the title track as racist and sexist, the most offensive of the suggestions being that 'black girls just want to get fucked all night.' Racism was an unlikely charge to bring against the likes of the Stones, who constantly acknowledged their debt to the black music scene, but Jagger's attitude towards women had not improved over the years. This followed hot on the heels of

feminist outrage over the cover of BLACK AND BLUE, which showed a woman in torn clothes tied with rope and heavily bruised.

The successor to SOME GIRLS, the album EMOTIONAL RESCUE, released in June 1980, was also a disappointment. The title track, released as a single, has Jagger singing falsetto to a disco rhythm, which is initially entertaining but ultimately rather bland. Other tracks are standard Stones numbers, driven by the trademark guitar riffs, but lacking the power and purpose of their other work. DOWN IN THE HOLE, a good track which took them back to their blues roots, served to remind us of what was missing. In short, the album lacked the raw energy of the previous release. Nevertheless, it reached No. 1 on both sides of the Atlantic, although this was probably due to the success of the previous album. Some albums, such as BEGGAR'S BANQUET, had done badly to begin with because at the time of release the Stones' career was at a low point, and they followed albums which were judged to be poor. In this case the success of the previous album meant that expectation was high, and the album quickly reached the top of the charts, although in later years it was to be disregarded in favor of more mature and rounded albums.

In 1981 the Stones again returned to touring with the release of the album TATTOO YOU. Confirmation of Ron Wood's growing influence in the group was provided in that two of the tracks were credited to Jagger/Richards/Wood. Another two were tracks originally recorded in 1972, and two more dated from 1975 recording sessions in Rotterdam. Hardly surprising, then, that while the album was competent, it contained nothing new. It was generally preferred to the previous album, but was still what was becoming a standard

impetus and inspiration provided by Richards' and Jagger's meeting. The old magic is clearly rekindled in this album. Another interesting feature is the use of the Master Musicians of Joujouka, a band of drummers and pipers from Morocco whose music had so fascinated Brian Jones back in 1968, when he had made a recording of their songs which was

issued on the Rolling Stones label a few years after his death. Their contribution can be heard on the track CONTINENTAL DRIFT, one of the more unusual tracks on the album.

The tour of North America followed. Announced in July of that year, ticket sales had broken all previous records. Fans paid up to $1000 for $25 tickets in some venues, and the tour was the biggest grossing tour in history at over $110 million. The European leg of the tour the following year grossed over £50 million in ticket sales and merchandising, this time sponsored by Budweiser. Concerts for the North American tour lasted for over two hours, and finished with SATISFACTION. JUMPIN' JACK FLASH was generally reserved for an encore. The set itself was even more lavish; built to reflect a mood of urban decay, it included a series of video screens to enable the huge crowd to see what was happening on the stage more clearly, and occasionally to carry early footage of the Stones to complete the performance. It was certainly a part of the by now expected spectacle of rock'n'roll, but critics everywhere clearly found it difficult to criticize; indeed, praise was lavished on them. This time they seemed to have got it right; they had built a truly entertaining show for the fans, but had managed to dispense with the kind of arrogance which had marked some previous occasions. At one point Jagger even asked the crowd if they minded a few songs from the new album. But

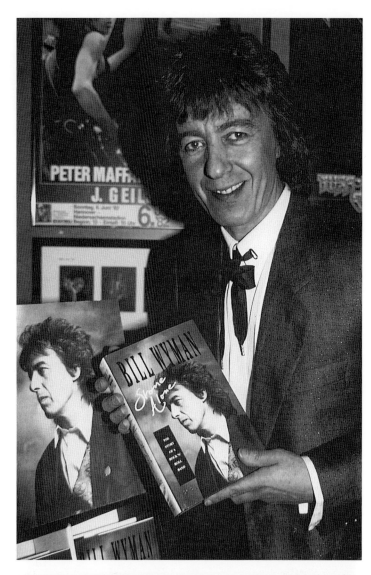

Left: **Family man Jagger with his entourage. Left to right: Karis, daughter by Marsha Hunt, carrying Elizabeth, first child by Jerry Hall, next to Jade. And nanny makes seven, pushing the son and heir, seven-month-old James.**

Right and below: **While differences kept the Glimmer Twins apart, the other Stones gathered no moss. Wyman brought out his autobiography, and Watts got back to his roots touring with the Charlie Watts Orchestra.**

Left: **The stage sets have become ever more lavish with the passing years. Yards of scaffolding and acres of lighting are now complemented by a giant inflatable doll.**

Below left: **Hope I die before I get old. The Stones, representatives of a generation who once thought no one over 30 could be trusted.**

Above: **Assembled in Grand Central Station to announce their tour to promote the Steel Wheels *album.***

Below: **The Stones' audiences now comprised a comprehensive mix of age ranges, from die hards to youngsters on their first visit.**

the crowd, many of them as old as the Stones themselves, didn't seem to mind at all.

At a time when various of the super groups were making comebacks, among them Bob Dylan, Jefferson Airplane and The Who, all grossing huge sums from world tours, cynics could be forgiven for wondering if money was the prime motive. But looking around the audience, composed variously of middle-aged business executives and punk rockers alike, there would be few who would not think the performance worth every penny. Another more pressing question concerned exactly how much longer the Stones could be expected to continue. However, they were all keen to dismiss suggestions that they were too old during the last tour over seven years ago, and Wyman celebrated his 53rd birthday midway through this tour. No matter how impressive the performance, it has been suggested that the Stones should quit while they're ahead. But Richards could never accept that. In an interview with Rolling Stone he commented, 'I can never think of starting something up again just to make it the last time. This is the beginning of the second half.' If this is true, then Wyman will be 83 before he retires. Will they still be known then as the bad boys of rock'n'roll?

Far left: *Richards, the rock survivor par excellence. In July 1974 he was nominated by* New Musical Express *readers 'The World's Most Elegantly Wasted Human Being.' After many years in the wilderness due to drugs and feuds with Jagger he seems, finally, to have come through intact.*

Below left: *Bill Wyman's marriage to model Mandy Smith was destined not to last. In 1993, after their divorce, both remarried.*

Left: *Charlie Watts*

Left: **The Rolling Stones announce their Voodoo Lounge tour and album to the world's press in New York, May 1994. Bassist Darryl Jones, who has played with Madonna, Sting and Miles Davis, has been brought in to replace Bill Wyman.**

Right: **The four remaining Stones sail up New York's Hudson River on board the Honey Fizz – once owned by President Kennedy – before detailing their tour plans.**

STUDIO ALBUMS

The Rolling Stones	April 1964*
The Rolling Stones:	
England's Newest Hit Makers	May 1964†
12 × 5	October 1964†
Rolling Stones No. 2	January 1965*
The Rolling Stones, Now!	February 1965†
Out of Our Heads	July 1965†
	September 1965*
December's Children	November 1965†
Aftermath	April 1966*
	June 1966†
Between The Buttons	January 1967
Their Satanic Majesties Request	November 1967†
	December 1967*
Beggar's Banquet	November 1968†
	December 1968*
Let It Bleed	November 1969†
	December 1969*
Sticky Fingers	April 1971
Exile On Main Street	May 1972
Goat's Head Soup	August 1973
It's Only Rock'n'Roll	October 1974
(Metamorphosis)	(June 1985)‡
Black and Blue	April 1976
Some Girls	June 1978
Emotional Rescue	June 1980
Tattoo You	August 1981
Undercover	November 1983
Dirty Work	March 1986
Steel Wheels	August 1989†
Urban Jungle	September 1989*

LIVE ALBUMS

Got Live If You Want It!	November 1966†
'Get Yer Ya-Yas Out'	
The Rolling Stones in Concert	September 1970
Love You Live	September 1977
Still Life	June 1982

COMPILATION ALBUMS

Milestones	Dec 1971 (Europe only)
Big Hits	
(High Tide and Green Grass)	March 1966†
	November 1966*
Flowers	June 1967†
Through The Past Darkly	
(Big Hits Vol. 2)	September 1969
Hot Rocks: 1964-1971	December 1971†
More Hot Rocks	
(Big Hits & Fazed Cookies)	December 1972†
Made In The Shade	June 1975
The Rolling Stones Greatest Hits	
Vols. 1 and 2	August 1977†
Get Stoned	November 1977*
Time Waits For No-One	June 1979*
Sucking In The Seventies	March 1981†
	April 1981*
Rewind (1971-1984)	June 1984*
	July 1984†
The Rolling Stones Singles Collection:	
The London Years	August 1989†

‡Unofficial compilation of early and previously unreleased material
†US only *UK only

INDEX

Page numbers in *italics* are illustrations.

'Aftermath' 20, 25, 26, 34
Altamont 38, 42, *42*, 47
'Angie' 47
'Around And Around' 51
'As Tears Go By' 25
Atlantic Records 44, 47, 49

'Back Street Girl' 27
Bailey, David 15, 18
Baker, Ginger 6
Baldry, Long John 6
Bangor, North Wales *32*
Barber, Chris 10
Beach Boys 16, 33
Beatles, the 10, 18, 33, 44
'Beatles For Sale' 16
Beck, Jeff 6, 49
'Before They Make Me Run' 51
'Beggar's Banquet' 35, *36*, 38, 42, 44, 53
'Be My Baby' 12
Berry, Chuck 6, *8*, 10, 12, 15, 16, 18, 51
'Between The Buttons' 25, 26, 33
Block, Judge 26, 30, 33
Blues Incorporated 6
Bowie, David *48*, 54
'Bright Lights, Big City' 6
Brown, James 16
Brown, Ollie 52
Browne, Tara 25
Bruce, Jack 6
'Bye Bye Johnny' 12

Cheltenham 6, 40
'Cherry Oh Baby' 49
Chess studios 15, 16
Chicago 15, 24
Chicago Sunday Times 46
Chichester Magistrates Court 31
Clapton, Eric 6
'Come On' 10
'Continental Drift' 56
Crawdaddy Club, the 10
Crosby, Stills, Nash and Young 38

'Dancing In The Street' 54
Decca 10, 12, 18, 20, 36
Degree Of Murder, A 38
Diddley, Bo 10, 12
Dirty Work 54
Dixon, Willie 15
Donaldson, Eric 49
'Down In The Hole' 53
Drifters, The 18
Dylan, Bob 54, 60

Ealing Blues Club 6
Ed Sullivan Show, The 16, *16*, 25, *26*
'Emotional Rescue' 53
'Empty Heart' 15
European tour *16*, 19
'Exile On Main Street' 44, 47

Faces, The 49
Faithfull, Marianne 25, 26, *31, 32*, 38, *40*
'Far Away Eyes' 53
'Fool To Cry' 49
France 44
Fraser, Robert 25, 28, 30

Gallagher, Rory 49
Gather No Moss 16
'Get Off Of My Cloud' 20, 23, 26
Gimme Shelter 41, 48
'Goat's Head Soup' 47
Godard, Jean-Luc *36*
Gomelsky, Giorgio 10

Grateful Dead 38

Hall, Jerry *57*
'Harlem Shuffle' 54
Harrison, George 10
'Have You Seen Your Mother Baby, Standing In The Shadow' 24, 26, *26*
'Heart Of Stone' 16
Hell's Angels 38, 41, 42
Help! 20
Holly, Buddy 12
'Honky Tonk Women' 38
Hunt
  Karis 57
  Marsha 57
Hunter, Meredith 41
Hyde Park 38, *41*

'In Another Land' 34
'It's All Over Now' 15
'It's Only Rock'n'Roll' 47
'I Wanna Be Your Man' 10

Jackson, Jesse 53
Jagger
  Elizabeth 57
  Jade 57
  James 57
  Mick 6, *8*, 10, 12, *13, 14*, 16, 19, *19*, 20, 23, *24*, 25, 28, 30, *31, 32*, 34, 35, *35*, 36, 38, 40, 44, 47, *47*, 48, 49, *51, 52*, 53, 56, 57, *58*
Jefferson Airplane 38, 41, 60
JFK stadium 54
John Mayall's Bluesbreakers 38
Jones, Brian 6, *8, 9, 10, 13*, 19, 25, *26*, 28, 30, *31, 32, 35, 36*, 38, *40*, 41, 56
'Jumpin' Jack Flash' 35, 38, 42, 57

Klein, Allen 20, 23, 33, 44
Komer, Alexis 6

'Last Time, The' 19, 30
Lennon, John 10, 12
'Let It Bleed' 42, 44
'Let's Spend The Night Together' 25
Little Boy Blue and the Blue Boys 6
'Little By Little' 12
'Litle Red Rooster' 16, 18, 51
Little Richard 6, *8*, 10
Live Aid 48, 54
Los Angeles Forum 38

de Macias, Bianca Perez Moreno 44, *47*
Madison Square Gardens 38, 54
Mandel, Harvey 49
Marquee, the 6, *9*
Marriott, Steve 49
Master Musicians of Joujouka 56
Maysles
  Albert 41, *42*
  David 41, *42*
McCartney, Paul 10, 12
Melody Maker 15
'Midnight Rambler' 42
Miller, Jimmy 35
'Miss You' 53
'Money' 12

New Musical Express 12, 20, 61
  Pollwinners' Concert 35
News of the World 28
Newsweek 23
New York 15, 24, 26, 44
'Not Fade Away' 12

'Off The Hook' 16, 18
Oldham, Andrew 10, 12, *13*, 15, 18, *18*, 20, 24, 25, 33
One Plus One 36
'Out Of Our Heads' 20

Pallenberg, Anita 25, 28, *35*, 38, 44, 47, 51
Paris 28, 44
Perkins, Bill see Wyman
Perkins, Wayne 49
Pitney, Gene 12, 13
'Play With Fire' 19
'Poison Ivy' 10
Preston, Billy 52

RCA studios 20
Ready, Steady, Go! 13, 14, 26
Rees-Mogg, William 30
Rewind 54
Richards, Keith 6, *8*, 10, 12, *13*, 16, *16, 18*, 19, 20, 23, 25, 28, 30, *31, 35*, 35, 38, 44, *47*, 49, 51, *51*, 52, 54, 56, 60, 61
Robinson, Smokey 16
Rock'n'Roll Circus 36
Rolling Stone magazine 20, 42, 60
'Rolling Stones No. 2' 16
Ronettes, The 12
Ronson, Mick 49
Royal Albert Hall 31
'Ruby Tuesday' 25
Rudge, Peter 44

San Bernardino 23
San Francisco 38
Santana 38
'Satisfaction (I Can't Get No)' 20, 23, 26, 35, 57
Schatzberg, Jerry 25
Schlöndorff, Volker 38
Scully, Rock 42
'Sergeant Pepper's Lonely Hearts Club Band' 33, 34
'She's A Rainbow' 34
'She's The Boss' 54
Shrimpton
  Chrissie 25
  Jean 25
'Slow Time Waits For No-One' 47
Smith, Mandy *61*
'Some Girls' 51, *51*, 53
Spector, Phil 12
Spencer Davis Group 35
'Star' 47
Station Hotel, Richmond 10

'Steel Wheels' 59
Stewart, Ian 10, 54
Stewart, Rod 49
'Still Life' 54
'Sticky Fingers' 44
Sunday Night At The Palladium 27
'Sympathy For The Devil' *36, 38*, 41

'Talk is Cheap' 54
'Tattoo You' 54
Taylor, Dick 6
Taylor, Mick 38, *41*, 48, 49
'Tell Me (You're Coming Back)' 12
'That Girl Belongs To Yesterday' 12, *13*
'Their Satanic Majesties Request' 33, 34, *35*, 42
'Through The Past Darkly' 34, 38
Times, The 30
Top of the Pops 24
Tour of the Americas 52
Turner, Tina 54
'2000 Light Years From Home' 34

'Undercover' 54
'Under My Thumb' (recording by The Who) 30
'Under The Boardwalk' 18
United States 15, *16*, 19, 25, 38, 56, 57

Warhol, Andy 44
Waters, Muddy 6, 12, 15, 18
Watts, Charlie 6, *8, 16*, 24, 38, 57, 61
  Charlie Watts Orchestra 54, 57
Who, The 28, 60
Wilson, Brian 33
Womack, Bobby 15
Wood, Ron 48, 49, *51*, 51, 52, 54
Wyman, Bill 6, *8, 9*, 16, *16*, 19, *23*, 34, 44, 47, 57, 60, 61

Yogi, Maharishi Mahesh 32
'You Better Move On' 12
'You Can't Always Get What You Want' 38

Zurich 28, *31*

ACKNOWLEDGMENTS

The author and publisher would like to thank the following for their help in the preparation of this book: Alan Gooch the designer, Judith Millidge the editor, Nicki Giles for production, Sara Dunphy for picture research.

We are also grateful to the following agencies for use of the pictures on the pages noted below:

Bettmann Archive: pages 4-5, 8 (top), 16 (both), 19 (both), 26, 27 (below), 30 (both), 31 (top), 34, 39, 40 (below), 41 (below), 49 (both), 61 (below), 51, 59 (top).
Brompton Picture Library: pages 7, 17 (top), 28 (left), 32, 33 (both), 42, 43 (both), 48 (top), 55 (top).
Globe: pages 18 (left), 23, 35, 40 (top), 46 (top), 47 (top), 56, 61
Dave Bennett/Globe: page 57 (top).
Patrick Lichfield/Globe: page 47.
Richard Open/Globe page 60 (below).
Graham Wiltshire/Globe: pages 51, 58 (top).
Photofest: pages 39, 46 (below), 47 (below), 52, 53.
Pictorial Press: pages 9 (top), 11, 12, 13 (both), 14 (below), 15 (both), 18 (right), 22, 25, 27 (top), 31 (below), 36, 37, (top), 41 (top), 48 (below), 50, 60 (top).
Jordan/Pictorial Press: page 9 (below).
Rex Features: pages 8 (below), 17 (below), 29, 37 (below), 45, 55 (main picture), 62, 63.
Eugene Adebari/Rex: pages 57 (below), 59, 62, 63.
Claude Gassian/Rex: page 58 (below).
Hoffman/Rex: page 14 (top).
Terry O'Neill/Rex: page 21.
Marc Sharratt/Rex: page 24-25.